ISBN 978-0-266-06337-7
PIBN 10947798

This book is a reproduction of an important historical work. Forgotten Books uses
state-of-the-art technology to digitally reconstruct the work, preserving the original format
whilst repairing imperfections present in the aged copy. In rare cases, an imperfection in
the original, such as a blemish or missing page, may be replicated in our edition. We do,
however, repair the vast majority of imperfections successfully; any imperfections that
remain are intentionally left to preserve the state of such historical works.

English
Français
Deutsche
Italiano
Español
Português

www.forgottenbooks.com

Mythology Photography **Fiction**
Fishing Christianity **Art** Cooking
Essays Buddhism Freemasonry
Medicine **Biology** Music **Ancient**
Egypt Evolution Carpentry Physics
Dance Geology **Mathematics** Fitness
Shakespeare **Folklore** Yoga Marketing
Confidence Immortality Biographies
Poetry **Psychology** Witchcraft
Electronics Chemistry History **Law**
Accounting **Philosophy** Anthropology
Alchemy Drama Quantum Mechanics
Atheism Sexual Health **Ancient History**
Entrepreneurship Languages Sport
Paleontology Needlework Islam
Metaphysics Investment Archaeology
Parenting Statistics Criminology
Motivational

Foreign
OPS AND MARKETS

(FOR RELEASE MONDAY, JANUARY 24, 1955)

VOLUME 70   NUMBER 4

CONTENTS

UNITED STATES DEPARTMENT OF AGRICULTURE
FOREIGN AGRICULTURAL SERVICE
WASHINGTON 25, D.C.

LATE NEWS

Cotton mill consumption in Canada during December 1954 amounted to 32,000 bales (500 pounds gross) an increase of 10 percent over 29,000 bales consumed in November and 28 percent higher than December 1953. Recent reports of increased activity in the cotton textile industry indicate that improvement may continue for the next few months. The total for August-December 1954 is 145,000 bales as compared with 134,000 for a corresponding period a year ago.

- - - - - - - - - - - -

Cotton consumption in Western Germany in October 1954 amounted to 110,000 bales (500 pounds gross), dropping 5 percent from September, but approximately the same as October 1953. Consumption for the August-October 1954 quarter was 319,000 bales or about 7 percent more than in the similar period a year ago. Cotton imports for August-October 1954 amounted to 278,000 bales or 3 percent more than in the comparable quarter in 1953. The United States' share of imports in the current period increased to 79,000 bales or 28 percent of the total, as compared with 44,000 bales or 16 percent of the total a year ago.

- - - - - - - - - - - -

Recent reports on the 1954-55 cotton crop in Pakistan indicate that yields are running below earlier expectations, and that the total crop may not exceed 1,225,000 bales (500 pounds gross), only slightly above the 1953-54 crop of 1,215,000 bales. Early arrivals of the varieties 289F and 4F indicate a crop of about average quality, though somewhat more stains than last year were noticeable. The 289F crop was generally of good staple but somewhat dull in color. The Punjab Desi crop was reportedly inferior in comparison with last year's crop.

- - - - - - - - - - - -

(Continued on Page 104)

FOREIGN CROPS AND MARKETS

Published weekly to assist the foreign marketing of U. S. farm products by keeping the nation's agricultural interests informed of current crop and livestock developments abroad, foreign trends in production, prices, supplies and consumption of farm products, and other factors affecting world agricultural trade. Circulation is free to persons in the U. S. needing the information it contains.

Foreign Crops and Markets is distributed only upon a request basis. Should you find you have no need for this publication, please tear off the addressograph imprint with your name and address, pencil "drop" upon it, and send it to the Foreign Agricultural Service, Room 5922, U. S. Department of Agriculture, Washington 25, D. C.

DEMAND FOR PRUNES IN THE
U.K. AND WEST GERMANY

The United Kingdom and Western Germany are important markets for dried prunes. The principal suppliers of these prunes are the United States and Yugoslavia. Prior to World War II, the United States shipped about 21,000 short tons annually to the United Kingdom, and about one-fourth of the 20,000 tons imported by the Germans. In 1953-54, approximately 15,000 tons of United States prunes were shipped to the United Kingdom under Section 550. Despite the increase in population, it has been difficult disposing of the smaller quantity of prunes in the United Kingdom markets.

The British prefer the large-size prunes, mostly from 30 to 60 sizes. However, most of the 1953 United States shipments consisted of small prunes. The larger sizes in these shipments moved out quickly, but many of the smaller prunes remained in storage. These prunes were purchased by the Ministry of Food, and arrived on the United Kingdom market during a short period of time. If purchases had been made by the trade, it is likely that shipments would have been spread over a longer period, and they may have purchased the more preferred sizes.

During the past two years, Yugoslavia has actively entered the United Kingdom market for prunes. Consumers in the United Kingdom prefer California prunes over those from other countries. The Yugoslav prunes are well packaged and are nicely faced, but the trade reports they lack keeping quality. Also, the prunes are sticky and have a smoky flavor, evidently caused by the drying process. The Yugoslav and United Kingdom traders have not been able to establish effective trading practices.

The United Kingdom market has been short of prunes for at least a decade, and many problems are being encountered in reestablishing this market. English consumers, as well as those in the United States, have a preference for more easily prepared desserts that require relatively little time in preparation. There have been few complaints relative to the price premium for California prunes in this quality-conscious market.

The West German market has been an important outlet for Yugoslav prunes, and there were few complaints on quality and flavor. In 1953, the United States supplied approximately one-third of the 4,300 short tons imported by the West Germans, who expressed the opinion that both the California and Yugoslav prunes are high in price by present standards.

The West German importers, due to geographic proximity, have better working relations with Yugoslavian exporters. Also, they personally visit the packing and shipping plants in Yugoslavia. The problems of increasing United States exports to Western Germany are likely to be greater than those for the United Kingdom market, even with a greater liberalization of trade with Western Germany.

SWEDEN REMOVES DOLLAR RESTRICTIONS
ON SOME FIELD SEED IMPORTS

Sweden on November 18, 1954 removed dollar restrictions on Grimm alfalfa, Kentucky bluegrass, meadow foxtail and colonial bentgrass seed for the current marketing season. However, quantitative controls are still in effect, according to the Agricultural Attache, American Embassy, Stockholm.

On the basis of present estimates wheat yields were at a near-record level, exceeded only in 1953. Yields of 42.6 bushels this year compare with the record of 44.9 bushels a year ago. Barley production, as now estimated at 105 million bushels, is also a near-record crop. Yields averaged 51.1 bushels per acre compared with the record yields of 52.9 bushels in 1953. Acreage, however, was about 8 percent below the level of the past 2 years.

Production of oats is now reported at 169.1 million bushels. This is 7 percent above the previous estimate, but is still somewhat less than production in recent years. The decrease from recent years is due to reductions in acreage as well as yields.

Fall sowing of grain for the 1955 harvest was hampered by excessive moisture, and conditions remained unfavorable through December in many areas. Early-sown grain was generally in good condition, according to a report on agricultural conditions at the beginning of January. Later-sown grain, however, was germinating slowly and unevenly. Some damage from waterlogging was also reported.

GERMANS REFUSE FRENCH BUTTER

A Paris newspaper reports that a German importer has recently refused delivery of 176,000 pounds of French butter because of failure to meet the specifications of the importer; the importer had requested delivery of white butter, but had been sent yellow butter. The newspaper cites this incident as an example of the need for the French exporter to be willing to meet the specifications of the importer. This is particularly important since France, with its current surplus problem, is trying to compete in the world butter market.

U. S. FURTHERS PORTUGUESE MILK QUALITY PROGRAM

Counterpart funds of the U. S. Foreign Operations Administration have been allocated to Portugal to help finance a Milk Quality Improvement Demonstration Program. Of the $50,000 allocated 25 percent of the funds were obligated for the purchase of washing tanks for 250 milk collecting stations. Disinfectants and detergents were also purchased for issuance to participating dairy farmers.

A number of veterinarians have already been employed and assigned to operational zones; also employed are several farm technicians. Laboratory testing of the milk has already begun.

The expenditure of Portuguese funds for livestock disease control work has been stepped up in the Lisbon milkshed as an integral part of the Milk Quality Improvement program.

DEMAND FOR PRUNES IN THE
U.K. AND WEST GERMANY

The United Kingdom and Western Germany are important markets for dried
prunes. The principal suppliers of these prunes are the United States and
Yugoslavia. Prior to World War II, the United States shipped about 21,000
short tons annually to the United Kingdom, and about one-fourth of the
20,000 tons imported by the Germans. In 1953-54, approximately 15,000 tons of
United States prunes were shipped to the United Kingdom under Section 550.
Despite the increase in population, it has been difficult disposing of the
smaller quantity of prunes in the United Kingdom markets.

The British prefer the large-size prunes, mostly from 30 to 60 sizes.
However, most of the 1953 United States shipments consisted of small prunes.
The larger sizes in these shipments moved out quickly, but many of the
smaller prunes remained in storage. These prunes were purchased by the
Ministry of Food, and arrived on the United Kingdom market during a short
period of time. If purchases had been made by the trade, it is likely that
shipments would have been spread over a longer period, and they may have
purchased the more preferred sizes.

During the past two years. Yugoslavia has actively entered the United
Kingdom market for prunes. Consumers in the United Kingdom prefer
California prunes over those from other countries. The Yugoslav prunes are
well packaged and are nicely faced, but the trade reports they lack keeping
quality. Also, the prunes are sticky and have a smoky flavor, evidently
caused by the drying process. The Yugoslav and United Kingdom traders have
not been able to establish effective trading practices.

The United Kingdom market has been short of prunes for at least a
decade, and many problems are being encountered in reestablishing this
market. English consumers, as well as those in the United States, have a
preference for more easily prepared desserts that require relatively little
time in preparation. There have been few complaints relative to the price
premium for California prunes in this quality-conscious market.

The West German market has been an important outlet for Yugoslav
prunes, and there were few complaints on quality and flavor. In 1953, the
United States supplied approximately one-third of the 4,300 short tons
imported by the West Germans, who expressed the opinion that both the
California and Yugoslav prunes are high in price by present standards.

The West German importers, due to geographic proximity, have better
working relations with Yugoslavian exporters. Also, they personally visit
the packing and shipping plants in Yugoslavia. The problems of increasing
United States exports to Western Germany are likely to be greater than those
for the United Kingdom market, even with a greater liberalization of trade
with Western Germany.

SWEDEN REMOVES DOLLAR RESTRICTIONS
ON SOME FIELD SEED IMPORTS

Sweden on November 18, 1954 removed dollar restrictions on Grimm
alfalfa, Kentucky bluegrass, meadow foxtail and colonial bentgrass seed
for the current marketing season. However, quantitative controls are still
in effect, according to the Agricultural Attache, American Embassy, Stockholm.

In addition to the foregoing items which are specifically opened to dollar imports, it was emphasized that other items might be eligible if desired by the trade.

This opening of the market to dollar imports is due in part to the very unfavorable harvest season and in part to the failure of French exporters to fulfill sales contracts.

Sweden, like other European countries, finds seed supplies both short and highpriced. Wholesale prices, in cents per pound, around the first of the year, were as follows: Late red clover 63 cents, medium late 64, early red 59, alsike 42, timothy 30, meadow fescue 39, orchardgrass 39 and black medic or yellow trefoil 31.

CUBAN RICE IMPORTS
DECLINE

Rice imports into Cuba during the July-December period of 1954 totaled 2,094,000 bags (100 pounds), according to data compiled from ships' manifests. This relatively small figure shows a reduction of 45 percent from imports of 3,774,000 bags in the corresponding months of the preceding rice-quota year (July-June). Virtually all rice imports in both years have been from the United States.

CUBA: Rice arrivals, by month, July 1952 to December 1954

July-June	1952-53		1953-54		1954-55	
	Monthly	Cumulative	Monthly	Cumulative	Monthly	Cumulative
	1,000 bags	1,000 bags	1,000 bags	1,000 bags	1,000 bags	1,000 bags
July	947	-	651	-	21	-
August	275	1,222	220	871	596	617
September	417	1,639	698	1,569	420	1,037
October	490	2,129	749	2,318	506	1,543
November	639	2,768	833	3,151	258	1,801
December	522	3,290	623	3,774	293	2,094
January	473	3,763	402	4,176	-	-
February	397	4,160	420	4,596	-	-
March	369	4,529	189	4,785	-	-
April	253	4,782	10	4,795	-	-
May	47	4,829	350	5,145	-	-
June	322	5,151	154	5,299	-	-

Compiled from ships' manifests.

CEYLON DOMESTIC RICE
SALES INCREASE

Rice consumption in Ceylon has increased by 400 long tons (900,000 pounds) a day since the doubling of the rice ration on November 8, according to a survey made by the Food Ministry. The survey, which was based on sales for one month, showed that average rice consumption has increased daily from 1,200 tons (2,700,000 pounds) to 1,600 tons (3,600,000 pounds). At the same time, the consumption of wheat flour has declined from 650 tons (1,450,000 pounds) to 580 tons (1,300,000 pounds) per day.

According to previous estimates of Ceylonese Government food officials, it was expected that because of the increase in rations, rice consumption would rise about 20 percent. Figures for one month, however, indicate a gain of 33 percent.

Official sources indicate that in the first 2 or 3 months of 1955, it is expected that rice consumption will probably level off, with a daily increase of about 20 to 25 percent, or 250 tons (560,000 pounds) to 300 tons (670,000 pounds). At this rate of increase, in one year, the gain would amount to around 100,000 long tons (220 million pounds) more than the average rice consumption before the rice ration was increased.

JAPAN-BURMA SIGN
1955 RICE CONTRACT

Japan on January 6 signed an agreement with Burma to purchase 220,000 metric tons (485 million pounds) of rice to be shipped by the middle of June 1955. Two stipulations of the agreement are that (1) a broken content of 15 to 25 percent will be allowed, depending on grade, and (2) the Burmese Government is to certify that all shipments are free of bacteria. The price varies according to the grade purchased, and is reported unofficially to average about 48L sterling ($6.00 per 100 pounds) f.o.b. Rangoon.

This contract is a continuation of the agreement entered into in 1954 covering a 4-year period, but requiring annual negotiations with respect to tonnage and price. The 1954 contract called for 300,000 metric tons (660 million pounds). This amount was shipped prior to the beginning of the monsoon season in order to avoid danger of deterioration.

U.K. REVISES
GRAIN ESTIMATES

Estimates of grain production in the United Kingdom have been revised and are now generally above earlier forecasts. The third official estimate of the season places wheat at 104.2 million bushels. This is slightly above the 1953 harvest of 99.5 million bushels and sharply above the 1945-49 average of 77.5 million.

On the basis of present estimates wheat yields were at a near-record
level, exceeded only in 1953. Yields of 42.6 bushels this year compare
with the record of 44.9 bushels a year ago. Barley production, as now
estimated at 105 million bushels, is also a near-record crop. Yields
averaged 51.1 bushels per acre compared with the record yields of 52.9
bushels in 1953. Acreage, however, was about 8 percent below the level
of the past 2 years.

Production of oats is now reported at 169.1 million bushels. This
is 7 percent above the previous estimate, but is still somewhat less than
production in recent years. The decrease from recent years is due to
reductions in acreage as well as yields.

Fall sowing of grain for the 1955 harvest was hampered by excessive
moisture, and conditions remained unfavorable through December in many
areas. Early-sown grain was generally in good condition, according to a
report on agricultural conditions at the beginning of January. Later-sown
grain, however, was germinating slowly and unevenly. Some damage from
waterlogging was also reported.

GERMANS REFUSE
FRENCH BUTTER

A Paris newspaper reports that a German importer has recently refused
delivery of 176,000 pounds of French butter because of failure to meet
the specifications of the importer; the importer had requested delivery
of white butter, but had been sent yellow butter. The newspaper cites
this incident as an example of the need for the French exporter to be
willing to meet the specifications of the importer. This is particularly
important since France, with its current surplus problem, is trying to
compete in the world butter market.

U. S. FURTHERS PORTUGUESE
MILK QUALITY PROGRAM

Counterpart funds of the U. S. Foreign Operations Administration have
been allocated to Portugal to help finance a Milk Quality Improvement
Demonstration Program. Of the $50,000 allocated 25 percent of the funds
were obligated for the purchase of washing tanks for 250 milk collecting
stations. Disinfectants and detergents were also purchased for issuance
to participating dairy farmers.

A number of veterinarians have already been employed and assigned
to operational zones; also employed are several farm technicians.
Laboratory testing of the milk has already begun.

The expenditure of Portuguese funds for livestock disease control
work has been stepped up in the Lisbon milkshed as an integral part of
the Milk Quality Improvement program.

SOUTH AFRICAN
WOOL MARKET

Wool sales in the Union of South Africa from the beginning of the
1954-55 season through November totaled about 125 million pounds,
greasy basis, as compared to 119 million for the corresponding period
of the 1953-54 season. The 1954 sales included about 6 million pounds
of Karakul wool while sales of a year earlier included 8 million
pounds of these wools.

Total receipts of wool for the 1954-55 season through November
were larger by 25 million pounds when compared with the same period of
the 1953-54 season. Stocks of unsold wool also were larger at the end
of November, 38 million pounds as compared to 26 million a year earlier.
The quantities of wool sold awaiting shipment totaled 49 million pounds
compared to 39 million at the end of November 1953.

Exports of greasy wool from July 1 to November 30, 1954 totaled
69.8 million pounds as compared with 70.4 million for the corresponding
period of 1953. The United Kingdom remained the largest and France
the second largest purchaser of South African wool, while Germany and
the United States each moved up one notch to third and fourth respectively.
Italy's position as an importer of South African wool declined from
third to fifth. The Soviet Union, with 1.3 million pounds purchased in
November, was the eight largest destination.

SOUTH AFRICA: Exports of Greasy Wool 1/
from July 1 to November 30, 1953 and 1954

Country of Destination	1953	1954	1954/1953
	Pounds	Pounds	Percent
United Kingdom	17,431,213	17,883,279	+ 2.6
France	15,508,523	13,314,419	- 14.1
Germany	10,219,582	13,183,951	+ 29.0
United States	7,776,145	6,984,196	- 10.2
Italy	11,197,410	6,493,694	+ 58.0
Belgium	5,814,987	4,376,819	- 24.7
Japan	803,230	3,388,325	+321.3
Soviet Union	0	1,282,595	-
Other	1,602,806	2,916,764	+ 82.0
Total	70,353,896	69,824,042	- 0.8

1/ Excludes scoured wool, wool tops and noils, and wooled sheepskin.
SOURCE: South African Wool Board.

In the last week of November the South African wool auction prices
rose to near the September opening level. Although prices were somewhat
weak and uneven no appreciable decline occurred in December and January
auction prices appear to be firm. The South African auctions opened
in September, 1954 with wool prices 15 to 18 percent below closing prices
in May. Prices rose about 5 percent during September, but by the end
of October prices were 2½ percent below the opening levels. These price
declines continued through the third week of November.

YUGOSLAVS RECEIVE U. S.
BUTTER GIFT

Stevedores worked around the clock last week so that Yugoslav flood victims could have United States butter on their bread and for cooking. More than 440,000 pounds of butter, the first consignment of a 1.65 million pounds donated to Yugoslav flood victims by President Eisenhower for the American people, was unloaded at Rijeka.

The speed in unloading was necessary since the flood area, Voivodine Province, is on the opposite side of Yugoslavia. The butter was unloaded from the United States refrigerator S. S. Exporter onto refrigerator rail cars, part of the 800 cars set aside for relief shipments by the Yugoslav government, for immediate shipment on the 600-mile journey.

The remaining 1.21 million pounds of United States butter is scheduled to arrive at the port of Rijeka on January 21 and 31. The wheat donation, made at the same time the butter was offered to the flood victims, arrived in Yugoslavia in the last week in December.

Distribution of the supplies is in the hands of the Yugoslav Red Cross.

BUTTER CONSUMPTION RISES
IN UNITED KINGDOM

The Commonwealth Economic Committee reports that butter consumption in the United Kingdom has increased almost 48 percent since derationing in May 1954. Average weekly consumption of butter in May was running around 11.3 million pounds, but during October had jumped to 16.7 million pounds. Sales of margarine, on the other hand, have risen only about 5 percent.

At least part of the gain in butter sales is attributed to the advertising program of the Danish, Australian and Dutch dairymen on the United Kingdom market (Foreign Crops and Markets, June 14, 1954). At the time of derationing the margarine advertising had been underway for some time, but the dairy program had not yet started. In June weekly sales of margarine were at a record 21 million pounds. With the stepped-up advertising of butter, and a drop in the butter price, margarine sales dropped and butter sales picked up. However, per capita butter consumption is still well below the prewar level of 24.8 pounds annually, while margarine, stimulated by wartime butter shortages, is more than twice prewar consumption rate of 10 pounds per person.

CATTLE EXPORTS
FROM PANAMA

Press reports indicate that several thousand head of beef cattle will be exported from Panama during the next few months and that export permits have already been granted for 1,000 head. Exports are controlled by the Panamanian Price Control Agency, by Resolution No. 79, of September 23, 1954. Panama has never exported large numbers of cattle.

Imports of live cattle from countries where foot-and-mouth disease is present have been prohibited since January, 1950, following an outbreak of the disease in Colombia, which was the most important import source for Panama.

Apparently demand for meat in Panama continues strong, despite reduced purchases by the Panama Canal Company in 1954. A temporary beef shortage in Panama City occurred in late 1954 when the largest slaughter house was closed, due to labor difficulties and the effects of the price controls on operating margins.

Since February 1951 fresh or frozen meat from countries having foot-and-mouth disease have been prohibited.

MEXICAN MEAT PACKING PLANTS
OPERATE AT LOW LEVELS

Only 2 of the 5 Federally inspected meat packing plants in the state of Chihuahua, Mexico, were in operation during December because of shortages of cattle. It is expected that the packing houses will operate at relatively low levels, at least until prices of cattle in Northern Mexico and in the United States become adjusted, now that exports to the United States are permitted.

One of the packing plants is expanding its pork business, is endeavoring to develop its markets for canned meat products and has engaged in chicken raising to diversify its activities. Another plant has less extensive diversification plans, although it is considering the purchase of cattle for feeding and export to the United States.

AIR-BEEF PROJECT LOSES
GOVERNMENT SUBSIDIES

The future of an experimental project for air freighting beef from inland stations in the Kimberleys, in Australia, is uncertain following withdrawal of State and Commonwealth Government subsidies. Air Beef was formed in 1949 by Kimberley station owners and 3 privately-owned airlines, to carry beef from an abattoir at Glenroy Station to the export packing plant at Wyndham. Subsidized to varying degrees from the start, it is questionable if it can survive without assistance.

A Commonwealth study in 1951 found the scheme dependent on the State Government's Wyndham Meat Works, which wraps and freezes carcasses and arranges export shipments. To support the venture, the State Government undertook to reimburse the company for part of the charges paid the Meat Works, while the Commonwealth paid the company a direct subsidy on the beef transported. Each Government has paid an average of about L10,000 a year under this agreement, which was to run for 4 years with possible renewal for two years.

In late October 1954 the State Cabinet announced its decision to discontinue the subsidy, stating that the company had received substantial financial help over a reasonable period. Since the Commonwealth payments had been contingent on the State Government's contribution, word quickly followed from Canberra that the federal subsidy would not be renewed.

An Air Beef panel has been appointed by the Commonwealth Government to study the general possibilities of air transport from inland slaughterhouses, with particular reference to the results of the scheme at Glenroy Station.

URUGUAYAN WOOL
CLIP LIGHTER

The 1954-55 Uruguayan wool clip was estimated earlier in the season at 210 million pounds or about 7 million pounds larger than last year's clip. Now with shearing completed the size of the clip is believed to be under that of the 1952-53 season, according to Dale Farringer, Agricultural Attache, American Embassy, Montevideo.

Although a precise production estimate is not available for the current season, wool deliveries to Montevideo warehouses indicate that the new clip may be from 2/10 to 9/10 pound per fleece lighter than last season. The lighter weights of these warehouse deliveries are attributed to slightly shorter staple length and less grease content. Also, the comparatively dry winter, over-crowded pastures, and the wide-spread presence of internal parasites are factors contributing to lower wool yields. The number of sheep shorn are believed to be about the same as a year ago, 28.3 million head.

SPANISH TOBACCO PRODUCTION
SPREADING TO A NEW AREA

The American Consulate at Bilbao, Spain reports an attempt is being made to increase production of tobacco along the Bay of Biscay coast in northern Spain. Reports indicate that the new area has gained a sizable group of tobacco growers and is being encouraged by the provincial government. Government aid is being given in the form of credit for dryer construction, cooperative seed plots, and assistance in getting their tobacco varieties classified by Spanish National Tobacco Service.

SOUTHERN RHODESIA'S TOBACCO PRODUCTION 1/
SETS RECORD IN 1954

The American Consul General at Salisbury reports that 1954 was a record year for flue-cured tobacco. Auction sales totaled 120.3 million pounds with a value of 53.5 million dollars. Increased yields per acre more than offset a slightly lower average price as shown in the following comparison of the past 5 years:

1/ A detailed background of the tobacco situation in the Rhodesian Federation can be found in Foreign Agriculture Circular FT 36-54.

Year	Sold at Auction	Value 1/	Average Price Per Pound	Acres Planted	Average Yield Per Acre
	1,000 pounds	1,000 dollars	U. S. cents	1,000 acres	pounds
1950 ....:	104,216	45,654	43.72	153	683
1951 ....:	89,474	35,911	40.13	168	533
1952 ....:	96,578	48,034	49.73	189	511
1953 ....:	105,152	48,478	46.10	177	594
1954 ....:	120,251	53,544	44.53	173 2/	697 2/

1/ Converted on the basis of $2.79 per Southern Rhodian ₺.
2/ Estimated.

The final purchases by markets were as follows:

Market	1953	1954
	1,000 pounds	1,000 pounds
United Kingdom ....:	59,384	69,653
Australia ....:	8,323	10,057
Local Markets ....:	5,974	6,833
Other Markets ....:	31,315	33,676
Unallocated ....:	155	32

The 1955 tobacco crop, marketing of which will begin in late March, has been damaged by heavy rains. Early estimates that placed the crop at a probable 115.5 million pounds have been revised to 106.0 million pounds. Possible damage to quality of the remaining crop cannot be estimated this early.

The quality of the major portion of the 1954 crop was considered improved in both texture and body over previous crops. There were 59 million pounds of well-bodied leaf grades in this crop compared with an average of 42 million pounds during the previous 6 seasons. This was especially important in view of the emphasis that had been placed on British needs for well-bodied leaf instead of thin, highly-colored types by the Tobacco Advisory Committee of the United Kingdom.

DENMARK MAY LIBERALIZE
IMPORTS OF DOLLAR TOBACCO

A recent statement by the Danish Minister of Commerce reported a list of commodities upon which dollar restrictions will be eased considerably. Among the commodities receiving preliminary consideration was unmanufactured tobacco. Final action is expected some time during this month.

IMPORTS OF CATTLE FROM
MEXICO REACH 54,000

About 54,000 cattle from Mexico entered the United States during the
two weeks ended January 15--the first importations since the Mexican-
United States border was closed on May 23, 1953--according to reports from
border inspectors of the U. S. Department of Agriculture's Agricultural
Research Service. Imports during the week ended January 15 totaled
around 30.000 head.

EXPORTS OF U.S. DRY EDIBLE
PEAS AT HIGH LEVEL

United States exports of dry edible peas during August-October 1954,
the first quarter of this marketing year, totaled 322,000 bags. These
were the largest exports for the first quarter of any marketing season
since 1949. They compare with 115,000 bags exported in the first quarter
of last year, and 120,000 bags the year previous. Exports in October
alone were 234,000 bags, the largest for any one month in the past 5
years. The previous record was 288,000 bags exported in September 1949.

Most of the increase occurred in exports to Continental Europe and
Colombia, South America. The Netherlands, Belgium, and West Germany,
were the largest importers in Europe, with each purchasing 30,000 to
80,000 bags in this quarter. Norway, Switzerland, and Czechoslovakia,
also took large increases, but the quantities were relatively small.

Poor harvest weather which did considerable damage in the pea-growing
areas of Europe, was a major cause of increased exports to that area.
Production in Europe, although of poor quality this year, was larger than last
season in most countries. Only the United Kingdom reported a decline in
the quantity produced. Data on production of dried peas were published
in Foreign Agriculture Circular FV 19-54 Prospects Good For Exports of Dry
Peas, November 24, 1954.

Europe, on the whole, has been a sporadic market for United States
peas, up one year and down the next. The Netherlands, Belgium, and
Western Germany, however, have each taken from 25,000 to 35,000 bags in
each of the last two seasons. In some seasons, these countries do not import peas from the United States. The Latin American countries, principally
Colombia, Cuba, and Venezuela, are steady customers for United States peas.

Colombia, usually an importer of small quantities of United States
peas, has broken all records this marketing season by importing 26,000 bags
in the first quarter, and 53,000 bags in the 6-months, May through October
of 1954. Colombia gives promise of becoming a large market for United
States peas, the trend being upward for almost two decades, and rapidly
upward in recent years.

The trend of United States pea exports to Venezuela has also been
upward, and steady. In the past 4 years they have varied between 100,000
bags and 180,000 bags per year. The 37,000 bags exported in the first
quarter of this year was 2,000 bags above the corresponding quarter of a
year ago.

Exports to Cuba, another steady and long-time market for United States peas, have been somewhat less this quarter than during the corresponding quarter in each of the 3 previous seasons. Cuba has purchased more than 100,000 bags from the United States during each of the past 2 years.

PEAS, DRY, EDIBLE: United States exports, first quarter
marketing seasons, 1948-49, 1954-55

(Marketing season begins August 1)

Country of destination	(100 pound bags)						
	1948-49	1949-50	1950-51	1951-52	1952-53	1953-54	1954-55
	1,000 bags	1,000 bags	1,000 bags	1,000 bags	1,000 bags	1,000 bags	1,000 bags
Canada ....:	2	4	24	27	5	3	2
Cuba ....:	20	18	25	52	34	42	27
Venezuela ....:	7	9	50	78	36	35	37
Colombia .....:	0	0	13	0	1	0	26
Belgium ......:	1	0	0	1	12	0	33
Netherlands ..:	2	0	3	0	5	6	60
W. Germany ...:	0	4	27	0	0	12	80
United Kingdom:	10	0	0	4	1/	1/	3
Norway ....:	0	0	0	0	0	0	5
Switzerland ..:	2	7	47	4	5	2	13
Czechoslovakia:	0	0	0	0	0	2	10
Other ....:	2/ 196	3/ 372	4/ 40	10	22	13	26
Total ......:	240	414	229	176	120	115	322

1/ Less than 500 bags.
2/ 146,000 bags to Austria and 41,000 bags to Japan.   3/ 348,000 bags to
Japan.
4/ 11,000 to Trinidad.

Source: Compiled from official sources.

VENEZUELA: SUGGESTED
EGG IMPORT RESTRICTIONS

One of Venezuela's large poultry feeders and egg producers, located near the Caracas market, is advocating compulsory branding of imported eggs and the application of the full duty of 27 cents per pound. This, he states, will increase the price of eggs by 42 cents per dozen and will bring the price of imported eggs within competitive range of local fresh eggs at $1.05 to $1.20.

The poultryman pointed out that the present situation with respect to local and imported eggs exactly parallels that of imported and local dressed poultry in 1949. When the Venezuelan Government took the advice of the poultrymen and prohibited imports, local production in time supplied the demand. He further suggested the same result would follow restricted egg imports.

To make this come true, the local hens would have to greatly increase production. In the case of poultry imports, imports of dressed poultry decreased after 1949, as imports of baby chicks increased. To have the same result with eggs, as imports of eggs are restricted, importation of laying chicks must increase. This is improbable in a short period, since Venezuela imported approximately 140 million eggs from the United States alone. This is the output of over 700,000 hens.

The Venezuela poultrymen are selling fresh eggs without difficulty in the price range of $1.05 to $1.20 per dozen. If imported eggs were forced off the market, the price of local eggs would most likely go back to that of the prewar days of $1.80 per dozen or more.

DECREASE IN BELGIUM'S
COTTON CONSUMPTION

Cotton consumption in Belgium amounted to 36,000 bales (500 pounds gross) in November 1954, a sharp decline from the two previous months, but higher than in November 1953, according to Robert N. Anderson, Agricultural Attache, Brussels. The several holidays in November were considered to be partly responsible for the drop from the high consumption rates in September and October. The monthly average for the August-November period was 39,000 bales as compared with the 12-month average of 36,000 for August-July 1953-54.

Belgium's cotton imports during August-October 1954 amounted to 106,000 bales, 13,000 less than consumption during this period and equal to imports for the corresponding period of 1953. No marked changes in sources of supply for the two periods were evident.

Belgium's cotton mill stocks on November 30, 1954, were reported at 133,000 bales, up about 6 percent from stocks of 126,000 bales held on July 31, 1954.

Fine cotton yarn production in November 1954 was reported at 7,681 metric tons as compared with 8,412 tons in October and 8,719 tons in September. Total yarn production for October was 10,179 tons, for September 10,397 tons. Total yarn production for November is not yet available.

BELGIUM: Imports of cotton from major countries of origin; averages
1934-38 and 1945-49; annual 1952 and 1953;
August-October 1953 and 1954

(Bales of 500 pounds gross)

Country of origin:	Year beginning August 1				August-October	
	Averages		1952	1953	1953	1954
	1934-38 1/	1945-49				
	1,000 bales	1,000 bales	1,000 bales	1,000 bales	1,000 bales	1,000 bales
Argentina......:2/	1	3/	23	27	10	8
Belgian Congo....:	120	85	57	72	23	20
Brazil..........:	26	32	3/	36	3	9
Egypt & Sudan....:	17	12	16	25	6	4
India & Pakistan.:	154	48	44	22	5	0
Mexico..........:	3/	:2/ 25	64	54	22	24
Peru............:	8	18	30	27	12	8
Turkey..........:	3/	:2/ 10	2	1	0	0
United States....:	145	130	114	101	12	13
Other countries..:	35	2	27	:4/ 99	13	:5/ 20
Total..........:	506	362	377	464	106	106

1/ Calendar years only available source.   2/ Two-year average.   3/ If any,
included in other countries.   4/ U.S.S.R. 29,000 bales.   5/ Guatemala and
Paraguay 5,000 each.

Source: Bulletin Mensuel du Commerce avec les Pays Etrangers;   Bulletin
Mensuel du Commerce Exterieur; reports from Agricultural Attaches
and other U. S. representatives abroad.

FRANCE CONTINUES INCREASED
COTTON IMPORTS

Imports of cotton into France amounting to 452,000 bales (500 pounds
gross) during August-November 1954 were 20 percent higher than in the comparable period of the previous year, according to Jeanne E. Charlot, American
Embassy, Paris. Increased imports were shown from all supplying areas, with
the exception of Egypt. The United States share of French cotton imports increased from 26 percent of the total in August-November 1953 to 31 percent of
the total for August-November 1954.

Cotton consumption in France during the 4-month period August-November
1954 amounted to approximately 436,000 bales or 4 percent above the total
for a comparable period a year ago. The monthly average for the current
period was 109,000 bales, as compared with the yearly average of 111,000
bales for August-July 1953-54 and 96,000 for the year 1952-53.

FRANCE: Imports of cotton from major countries of origin; average 1935-39; annual 1951-53; August-November 1953 and 1954

(Equivalent bales of 500 pounds gross)

Year beginning A

Country of origin	1,000 bales	1,000 bales	1,000 bales	1,000 bales	1,000 bales	1,000 bales
Argentina and Brazil	1/ 90	84	8	127	33	4
E. Equatorial Africa	22	2/	2/	2/	2/	2
Egypt	243	129	301	246	75	5
French Colonies	36	151	152	163	64	8
India and Pakistan	3/ 194	70	92	95	36	1
Mexico	2/	201	9	5	4/	
Peru	5/ 9	50 :6/	37 :6/	30 :6/	13	1
Turkey	2/ :7/	168 :7/	142 :7/	237 :7/	58 :7/	8
United States	669	353	523	480	96	14
Other countries	27	0 :8/	20	0	1	
Total	1,290	1,206	1,284	1,383		

1/ Brazil.   2/ If any, included in "Other countries."   3 British India. than 500 bales.   5/ 4-year average.   6/ Paraguay and Peru.   7/ Turkey, Uganda, Iran, and Syria.   8/ 13,000 bales from Sudan.

Source: Statistique Mensuelle du Commerce Exterieur de la France and reports f Agricultural Attaches and other U.S. representatives abroad.

      The number of active spindles was reported at 6,500,000 out of 7,600,000 spindles in place. Twister activity was 650,000 out of 800,000 in place. Of the 6,500,000 active spindles, 36 percent were operated one shift a day, 61 percent two shifts, and 3 percent 3 shifts. Of the 650,000 active twisters, 50 percent operated one shift a day, 46 percent two shifts, and 4 percent 3 shifts a day.

      Cotton stocks in France were reported at 365,000 bales on November 30, 1954, an approximate 3-month supply, and 23 percent higher than stocks of 296,000 bales held a year earlier. Stocks of United States cotton on November 30, 1954, were 94,000 bales or 26 percent of the total, as compare with 86,000 bales or 29 percent of the total held a year earlier. Percentages of other growths held on November 30, 1954, were as follows: Turkey and Syria 23 percent of the total; French Colonies 17 percent; Egypt 14 percent; Argentine and Brazil 12 percent; India-Pakistan 4 percent; Peru, Sea Island and Paraguay 3 percent; and Mexico 1 percent.

Prices established for December deliveries by the GIRC (Cotton Import and Distribution Office) in fulfillment of allocations, are shown below. Prices were quoted in French francs per kilogram (350 francs equal approximately $1.00), net weight, ex GIRC warehouse, and generally reflect the average price paid by GIRC for such growth during the preceding month.

Prices effective December 1, 1954 1/

	French francs per kilogram	Equivalent U.S. cents per pound
United States and similar growths:		
Strict Middling 1 inch rain-grown.......	325	42.12
Strict Middling 1-1/8 inch rain-grown ..	341	44.19
Egypt and similar:		
Fully Good Ashmouni 2 (medium staple),	403	52.23
Fully Good Giza 30 (medium staple).......	425	55.08
Fully Good Karnak 155 (long staple).....	520	67.39
Extra Karnak 151 (extra long staple)....	560	72.58
Sea Island:		
Antigua (extra long staple)............	650	84.24
India-Pakistan:		
Bengal Fine............................	281	36.42
Pakistan 289F, Medium RG/SG............	334	43.29

1/ Source: Bulletin Officiel des Services des Prix of December 11, 1954.

FORMATION OF COTTON PRODUCERS'
COOPERATIVE IN GUATEMALA

A cotton producers' cooperative association organized in Guatemala on December 10, 1954, includes practically all of the private cotton producers, according to C. T. Breaux and C. B. McKnight, American Embassy, Guatemala. This group accounts for about 60 percent of all cotton production. The remainder of the cotton is produced on farms under government control, but which may later be sold or leased to private interests.

Guatemalan cotton production has increased rapidly in recent years, from a 1945-49 average of 5,000 bales (500 pounds gross) to an estimated 16,000 bales in 1952-53, to 28,000 in 1953-54, and the current crop for the 1954-55 marketing year is expected to reach 40,000 bales. Approximately 12,000 bales are consumed annually, and the balance is available for export.

Exports during the 1953-54 crop year were estimated at approximately 21,000 bales, 16,000 from the 1953-54 crop, and 5,000 from the 1952-53 crop. This is the first year in which Guatemala has exported any cotton because production had never exceeded mill requirements until 1952-53. No cotton was exported in that year, however, because of high domestic prices, and the fact that Guatemalan cotton had not previously been classified according to international standards. The 1953-54 production was reported to be of very good grade, with a large part of staple lengths from 1-1/16 inches to 1-3/32 inches. Exports were principally of Strict Low Middling and Middling.

The newly organized cooperative which is known as the Association of Guatemalan Cotton Producers will provide marketing facilities for both cotton and cottonseed in domestic and international trade, and will supplant the Production Development Institute (INFOP) which had previously operated cotton marketing activities. The cooperative will also operate gins, provide grading facilities through the hiring of one or more foreign classifiers, and import insecticides, seeds and fertilizers. Plans are underway for the purchase of some 20 airplanes for dusting, and for a machinery pool for rent of equipment to cooperative members. The cooperative will serve as intermediary in obtaining bank credits for cotton producers, and will conduct research for the development of the cotton industry, and maintain statistics on production and trade.

Funds for operation of the cooperative will be obtained by a charge of 25 cents per quintal (101.4 pounds) of cotton ginned from the 1954-55 crop, the charge to be subject to annual revision. Cotton from Guatemala was not subject to export tax prior to October 19, 1954, when a tax of $2.00 per quintal (1.97 cents a pound) of ginned cotton was imposed on cotton exported from the 1954-55 crop. Although this was supposed to be a one-time tax, cotton producers feel that the increasing importance of cotton in the nations economy may result in continuation of the tax.

The current pricing system for cotton, which provides that the price of cotton placed in the railway station will follow international quotations as taken from the New York Cotton Exchange, was established by resolution of September 9, 1954. By the same action the Government abandoned its system in effect during 1953-54 of buying cotton at a fixed price and selling on the world market at losses ranging as high as 7.5 cents a pound.

CHINESE SOYBEANS, PEANUTS THROUGH
SUEZ CANAL UP SLIGHTLY

The northbound movement of Chinese soybeans through the Suez Canal in the first 10 months of 1954 totaled about 342,000 short tons (about 11,400,000 bushels), according to information available to the Foreign Agricultural Service. This quantity is slightly larger than shipments during January-October 1953. As in previous years, the average monthly rate of soybean movement in July-October was down sharply from the preceding 6 months. However, July-October shipments last year of some 52,000 tons (about 1,700,000 bushels) were nearly double those of the correspo period in 1953.

SUEZ CANAL: Northbound movement of vegetable oilseeds,
January-October 1954 with comparisons

(1,000 short tons, gross weight 1/)

Commodity	:Average: :1933-37:	1951	1952	1953 2/	January-October	
					1953 2/	1954 2/
Soybeans...............:	1,237:	551:	219:	353:	336:	342
Copra..................:	786:	1,066:	795:	660:	505:	689
Peanuts....ï...........:	999:	218:	207:	229:	201:	229
Cottonseed.............:	146:	195:	144:	197:	153:	132
Flaxseed...............:	227:	42:	34:	55:	48:	29
Other..................:	267:	224:	289:	417:	362:	281
Total oilseeds....:	3,662:	2,296:	1,688:	1,911:	1,605:	1,702

1/ Source data in 1,000 metric tons. 2/ Preliminary.

Source: Compiled from Le Canal de Suez Bulletin, Paris, France.

The volume of peanuts, mainly of Chinese origin, passing northward
through the Canal during January-October 1954 was about 14 percent larger
than in the first 10 months of 1953. Copra shipments, up 34 percent, were
largely responsible for the overall increase in the total northbound
movement of all oilseeds.

NIGERIA 1955 PRODUCER PRICES INTENDED TO
ENCOURAGE EDIBLE PALM OIL PRODUCTION

Although basic prices to be paid producers for palm oil in 1955 are
lower for all grades than in 1954, with the exception of Grade 2, Western
Region, a price differential in favor of Special Grades is continued.

Production of Special Grades of palm oil has been much less in the
Western Region than in the Eastern Region. The Western Region Marketing
Board established a price for Special Grade A (not over $3\frac{1}{2}$ percent free
fatty acid) which is $5 per short ton higher than the price established for
the Eastern Region. The price for Special Grade B (over $3\frac{1}{2}$ percent but
not over $4\frac{1}{2}$ FFA) is $10 per short ton higher than the price in the Eastern
Region.

Elbert R. Williams, American Consul, Lagos, recently reported that
Western Region officials stated they hope the higher price for Special
Grade oil will encourage producers to improve the quality so that more can
be graded as Special Grade A or B and less as Technical Grade 1 (not over
9 percent FFA).

The 1955 prices for the various grades of palm oil are shown in comparison with prices in 1950 through 1954 in the accompanying table.

NIGERIA: Producer prices for palm kernels and palm oil established by the Nigerian Marketing Boards, marketing seasons 1950-51 through 1954-55

(Dollars 1/ per short ton)

Commodity	Description	1950	1951	1952	1953	1954 2/	1955 Western Region 2/	1955 Eastern Region
Palm oil......:	Free fatty acid content							
Grades....								
Special 3/......:	Not over 4%	133	178	200	189	162	-	-
A.........:	Not over 3½%	-	-	-	-	-	150	145
B.........:	Over 3½% not over 4½%	-	-	-	-	-	130	120
Technical 1......:	Over 4½% not over 9%	107	138	152	145	125	112	95
2......:	Over 9% not over 18%	93	108	118	112	95	95	70
3......:	Over 18% not over 27%	83	85	88:4/	86:4/	82:4/	75:4/	50
4......:	Over 27% not over 36%	74	75	75	5/	5/	5/	5/
5......:	Over 36%	65	5/	5/	5/	5/	5/	5/
Palm kernels......:	Naked ex-scale port of shipment/bulk oil plant:	65	80	90	85	85	78	75

1/ Conversion rate - one British West African pound=U.S. $2.80. 2/ Subject to a Produce Sales Tax deduction of $2.50 per ton in the Western Region. 3/ There was only one grade of Special palm oil 1950 through 1954. 4/ The upper limit of grade 3 was raised to 30 percent FFA at the beginning of the 1953 season. 5/ Purchases discontinued.

Source: Annual reports of the Nigerian Marketing Boards and reports from the American Consulate General, Lagos.

NOTE: This table contains information in addition to that given in the similar table to be found in Foreign Crops and Markets for January 17, 1955. Prices for Special Grades of palm oil for the Western and Eastern Regions, which were transposed in the previous table, are correctly shown above.

PHILIPPINE COPRA EXPORTS
DROP IN DECEMBER

Philippine copra exports during December totaled 56,158 long tons, a decline of 15 percent from the previous month but 4 percent above the volume shipped in December 1953. Total shipments for the year 1954 amounted to 758,030 tons or 28 percent more than the 592,267 tons exported in 1953.

The breakdown of the December copra exports by country of destination is as follows: United States--18,003 (Atlantic-928, Gulf-1,896, Pacific-15,179); Canada--1,250; Belgium--1,200; Denmark--2,400; Germany--2,800; Italy--1,250; the Netherlands--12,900; Norway--500; Sweden--1,000; Europe unspecified--10,000; Iraq--1,000; Israel--1,000; and Colombia--2,855.

December exports of coconut oil amounted to 6,361 tons compared with 6,042 tons in November and 4,845 tons in December 1953. The January-December total was 65,732 tons against 58,589 in 1953. December shipments were as follows: United States--6,061 tons (Atlantic) and Cuba--300 tons.

On a copra equivalent basis, exports of copra and coconut oil for this year totaled 862,367 tons, or one-fourth more than the 685,265 tons exported in 1953.

The copra export price in mid-December was $175.00 per short ton, c.i.f. Pacific. Local buying prices in Manila were 30.00 to 31.50 pesos per 100 kilograms ($152.41 to $160.03) per long ton.

BURMA FORECASTS DROP
IN PEANUT OUTPUT

Burma's peanut production in 1954-55 is forecast at 179,000 short tons against 212,000 tons the previous year, reports James H. Boulware, Agricultural Attache, American Embassy, Rangoon. The planted area is estimated at 792,000 acres or 28,000 acres less than the 1953-54 acreage. Harvested acreage is estimated at 762,000 as compared with 794,000 a year ago. Due partly to the decrease in planted area, the primary factor in the estimated 15 percent decrease in anticipated production is the shortage of moisture in the producing districts.

INDIA ANNOUNCES FURTHER PEANUT OIL EXPORT
QUOTA; EXPORT DUTY ON CASTOR OIL REDUCED

The Government of India has announced further export quotas for peanut oil equal to individual shippers' exports during the period November 4, 1954, to January 20, 1955, reports the American Embassy, New Delhi. According to press reports, peanut oil quotas now total around 28,000 to 30,000 short tons to be shipped by the end of March. (See Foreign Crops and Markets of December 6, 1954, page 641, for previous announcements regarding peanut oil and castor oil quotas.)

At the same time, it was announced that the export duty on castor oil was reduced from 200 rupees to 125 rupees per long ton ($37.50 to $23.44 per short ton) effective immediately. The export duty on hand-picked selected peanuts, however, was raised from 150 rupees to 300 rupees per long ton ($28.12 to $56.25 per short ton). A further export quota for handpicked selected peanuts equal to 40 percent of shippers 1951, 1952, or 1953 exports also was granted. The volume of handpicked peanut exports is still highly problematical even though the quota now totals 80 percent of individual exporters' basic year exports.

Exports of ordinary peanuts from India is now prohibited.

WEST GERMAN TRADE TO IMPORT U.S.
LARD AGAINST FREE DOLLARS

The Government of Western Germany published on December 31, 1954, official invitations to German importers to import United States lard, both raw and purified (Stat. Tariff No. 1501: 11-21) against free dollars, reports John J. Haggerty, Agricultural Attache, Office of the U. S. High Commissioner for Germany, Bonn.

The lard so imported must be fresh and pure and of current production. Since the usual previous provisions for "lowest bids" are absent the importer is free to deal directly with a supplier of his own choice as to brand, quality and price. Initial individual licenses may be not less than 50,000 deutsche marks (about $11,900) nor more than 125,000 deutsche marks (about $29,800).

Contracts must be submitted for information purposes within 8 days and shipments must arrive within 50 days following issuance of license. On arrival, all lard first must be offered to the Import and Storage Agency for Fats and if not taken by that agency the lard can be sold commercially at the importer's risk.

ARGENTINA EXPORTS 5,100 TONS OF
TUNG OIL TO U.S IN OCT.-DEC.

Argentine exports of tung oil to the United States during the last 3 months of 1954 have been reported, unofficially as follows: October, 3,127 short tons; November, 1,317 tons; and December, 635 tons. The Governments of Argentina and Paraguay have agreed, respectively, to restrict their exports of tung nuts and oil to this country to 21.8 million pounds and 2.6 million pounds oil equivalent in the marketing year ending October 31, 1955. (See Foreign Agriculture Circular FFO 20-5', Fats and Oils Situation in Argentina, December 7, 1954, Note 5, page 6.)

LATE NEWS

Arrivals of cotton in Barcelona during the week of December 18-24, 1954 totaled 23,000 bales. An additional 97,000 bales have been purchased by the Center and are either on ships en route to, or awaiting early shipment to Barcelona. Thus the tight supply situation which appeared to be developing in the Spanish cotton mill industry near the end of 1954 has been relieved and a satisfactory supply situation is assured for the near future.

UNITED STATES DEPARTMENT OF AGRICULTURE
Washington 25, D. C.

Official Business

CPSIA information can be obtained
at www.ICGtesting.com
Printed in the USA
BVHW031146021118
531990BV00020B/1379/P